Creative Director: **Susie Garland Rice**
Graphic Design: **Melanie M. Lewallen**

Dalmatian Press owns all art and editorial material.
ISBN: 1-57759-258-1
© 1999 Dalmatian Press. All rights reserved.
Printed and bound in the U.S.A. The DALMATIAN PRESS name,
logo and spotted spine are trademarks of Dalmatian Press, Franklin, Tennessee 37067.
Written permission must be secured from the publisher to use or reproduce any part of this book.

10743a/Baby Animals

Baby animals

Illustrations: **Emily Owens**

Dalmatian Press

lamb

harbor
seal

koala bear

piglets

orangutan

elephant

raccoons

polar bear
cubs

wolf cubs

owlets